uides

nces

Australia

Make the most of your time on Earth

ROUGH GUIDES

25 YEARS 1982–2007

NEW YORK • LONDON • DELHI

Contents

Introduction

EXPERIENCES have always been at the heart of the Rough Guide concept. A group of us began writing the books **25 years ago** (hence this celebratory mini series) and wanted to share the kind of travels we had been doing ourselves. It seems bizarre to recall that in the early 1980s, travel was very much a minority pursuit. Sure, there was a lot of tourism around, and that was reflected in the guidebooks in print, which traipsed around the established sights with scarcely a backward look at the local population and their life. We wanted to change all that: to put a country or a city's popular culture centre stage, to highlight the clubs where you could hear local music, drink with people you hadn't come on holiday with, watch the local football, join in with the festivals. And of course we wanted to push travel a bit further, inspire readers with the confidence and knowledge to break away from established routes, to find pleasure and excitement in remote islands, or desert routes, or mountain treks, or in street culture.

Twenty-five years on, that thinking seems pretty obvious: we all want to experience something real about a destination, and to seek out travel's **ultimate experiences**. Which is exactly where these **25 books** come in. They are not in any sense a new series of guidebooks. We're happy with the series that we already have in print. Instead, the **25s** are a collection of ideas, enthusiasms and inspirations: a selection of the very best things to see or do – and not just before you die, but now. Each selection is gold dust. That's the brief to our writers: there is no room here for the average, no space fillers. Pick any one of our selections and you will enrich your travelling life.

But first of all, take the time to browse. Grab a half dozen of these books and let the ideas percolate … and then begin making your plans.

Mark Ellingham
Founder & Series Editor, Rough Guides

25

Ultimate
experiences
Australia

1
RAINFOREST VIBES: EXPERIENCE THE DAINTREE

Ancient rainforests cascading onto barely touched beaches, natural spa treatments, gourmet restaurants, beachside bungalows and world-class snorkelling on the Great Barrier Reef. The area around the Daintree River, between Port Douglas and Cape Tribulation in northern Queensland, is graced with some of the most spectacular landscapes, diverse flora and fauna, and unique eco resorts in Australia.

Part of the appeal is that Daintree's wild beauty has not been totally sanitized. Estuarine crocodiles still cruise among the mangrove swamps, the forests harbour plants with vicious stinging leaves, and the Coral Sea is home to box jellyfish, though fortunately only during the torpid wet season. Bright blue butterflies share the breeze with a variety of birds, from the giant, emu-like cassowary to kingfishers whose luminescent liveries will stop you in your tracks.

Decisions get no more fraught than choosing papaya or mango for breakfast or opting for either sustained relaxation or a bit of wilderness exploration. A wildlife-spotting boat trip up the Daintree River is a rewarding compromise, or a walk through the Mossman Gorge may give you an appetite for a crocburger (yes, it does taste like chicken). Alternatively, just head to the beach with a sarong and the latest copy of Australian *Hello* magazine. For the widest range of restaurants and cafés, base yourself in Port Douglas, also a good departure point for exploring the reef. Better still, push the boat right out and indulge yourself with a stay at the **Daintree Eco Lodge and Spa**. Set beside the river and surrounded by lush jungle, it offers exclusive treehouse accommodation and is renowned for its luxurious spa treatments. And there's no need to put ambient relaxation tunes on your iPod: the mellow sounds of the world's oldest living rainforest are music enough.

need to know
Daintree Village is a 110km drive north of Cairns, while Port Douglas a well-established holiday town 70km north of Cairns. Treehouses at **Daintree Eco Lodge** cost from Aus$500 per night (ⓦwww.daintree-ecolodge.com.au). **Cape Tribulation Beach House** (ⓦwww.capetribbeach.com.au) offers luxurious beachside bungalows for $180, or dorms for Aus$25.

2
discovering the secrets of

Kings Canyon

If you're looking for adventure amidst the awe-inspiring scenery of Australia's Red Centre, you'd be hard-pushed to find somewhere which can match the spectacle of Kings Canyon in Watarrka National Park. The pale orange walls of the sandstone canyon were carved out during a more humid climatic epoch, thousands of years ago. Today it lies in a scrubby semi-desert of scurrying lizards and gnarled trees.

The main attraction here is the six-kilometre walk taking you up

The main attraction here is the six-kilometre walk taking you up and around the canyon's rim. Along the way you'll uncover a variety of wildlife and their habitats, from rocky crevices to palm-filled gorges, and can wander off the track as close as you dare to the very edge of the 100m cliffs.

Early morning is the best time to head out, starting from the car park you begin with a 15-minute stepped ascent that will get your heart pumping. But don't be put off; at the top the worst is over and from here the trail leads through the "Lost City", a maze of sandstone domes where interpretive boards fill you in on the surrounding geology and botany.

Back on the signed track you clamber down into a palm-filled chasm which you cross via an impressive timber bridge. Spinifex pigeons and other birds dart overhead, while on the far side there's an easily missed ten minute detour downstream to a shady pool. Most tour groups are content to sit here, eating their snacks, but the highlight of the walk and a secret known to few, is looking out from the very throat of the canyon above a dry waterfall. You can get there either by wading knee-deep round the right bank of the pool, scrambling over the rock above, or simply gritting your teeth and swimming across. Peering from the brink you get a perfectly framed view of the sunlit south wall and the canyon far below. Returning to the bridge, the walk takes you back to the very rim of the overhanging south wall above the jumbled rocks, before descending gently back to the car park.

need to know

Kings Canyon is 400km from Alice Springs, on the way to Uluru. Allow about two and a half hours to enjoy the walk and take plenty of water. Ten kilometres past the canyon, you can camp, lodge and get fed at the **Kings Canyon Resort** (ⓦwww.kingscanyonresort.com.au).

3

What lies below

snorkelling at the
GREAT BARRIER REEF

"It's like being in another world!" may be the most predictable observation following a close encounter with the Great Barrier Reef, but it's only when you've come face to face with the extraordinary animals, shapes and colours found beneath the ocean's surface that you realize you've truly entered a watery parallel universe. And as a curious thick-lipped potato cod nudges your mask, you might also wonder, "who exactly

The Great Barrier Reef follows Australia's continental shelf from Lady Elliot Island, in southern Queensland, 2300km north to New Guinea. Its northern reaches are closer to land so, while it's 300km to the main body from Gladstone, Cairns is barely 50km distant, making this the best place for reef day-trips. Scuba diving may get you more quality time down below, but a well-chosen snorkelling location can reveal marvels no less superb without all the bother of training, equipment and lengthy

fety procedures. Though commonly lled the world's biggest life form, e Great Barrier Reef is more an tricate network of patch reefs than single entity. All of it, however, was ilt by one animal: the tiny coral olyp which grows together to create odular colonies – corals. These turn provide food, shelter and nting grounds for a bewildering ssortment of more mobile creatures.

Rays, moray eels and turtles glide effortlessly by, while fish so dazzling they clearly missed out on camouflage training dart between caves to nibble on coral branches, and slug-like nudibranchs sashay in the current. It all unfolds before you one breath at a time, a neverending grand promenade of the life aquatic.

need to know

A typical day trip from Cairns costs Aus$99 with lunch and three hours snorkelling. Don't forget a t-shirt to avoid sunburn, and for your sake and the coral's, look but don't touch.

4 Walking on the Wild Side at the Sydney Mardi Gras

The Sydney Gay & Lesbian Mardi Gras Parade is a party of the rarest and most uninhibited kind; it's the single largest night-time parade in the world and draws a bigger crowd than any other annual event in Australia, with about six thousand participants and half a million spectators. In essence, it's a full-on celebration of gay culture, and a joyous demonstration of pride; but it's enjoyable for people of any sexuality, provided partial nudity, g-strings, wild unleashings of inhibitions, senseless acts of kindness, random acts of love and lewd innuendo don't offend.

The parade route runs from Hyde Park, through the city's gay quarter, to Moore Park, and before the start the waiting crowd is whipped into a not-so-subtle frenzy over several hours by the presiding marshals. Searchlights, flares, fireworks, strobes and dance music from all the nearby clubs bring the throng to a fever pitch of anticipation – a perfect build-up to the gleaming Harley Davidsons of the Dykes on Bikes, who have heralded the start of the parade for many years. Vast floats, effigies and marching troupes follow in their wake – everything from two hundred drag Madonnas in cowgirl hats spilling out of the longest stretch limo you've ever seen, to three hundred Barbara Cartlands in pink-sequined evening gowns, or mist-enshrouded boats carrying Thai princes and princesses, to six hundred bootscooters of every gender, age and size.

Afterwards, Australia's biggest parade is followed by Australia's biggest party at Moore Park Entertainment Precinct. Tickets sell out fast, and scalpers loiter out the front touting tickets at exorbitant prices. Whatever your sexuality, it's a pretty decadent affair, and – how can we put this? – voyeurs are not en-couraged. But even if you can't get in, or just can't afford it, there are lots of places with plenty going on after the Parade. Just wander along the gay strip and the chances are you'll find every bar is jumping, and just as much fun as the last.

need to know

The Mardi Gras Parade is held on the evening of the first Saturday in March.
Full story at @www.mardigras.org.au.

5

WALK ROUND ULURU

As you cruise westwards along the Lasseter Highway, you get your first glimpse of Uluru over cinnamon-red dunes while still 50km distant. Slowly the ochre-coloured monolith invades the empty horizon; it's hard to look at anything else.

Then, just past the Uluru-Kata Tjuta National Park gates, you turn a bend, and suddenly it fills your field of vision. You simply have to stop and take a picture.

The Rock means different things to different people. To the Pitjanjarra people who've lived in its shadow for 20,000 years, "Uluru" is actually the name of a seasonal waterhole near the summit, formerly revealed only to initiates of the Mala wallaby clan during secret ceremonies. To them the mountain is no Mecca-like shrine, but a vital resource-rich landmark at the intersection of various trails in the region. These "songlines" criss-cross the desert and any conspicuous natural features found along them were put into songs celebrating the "Dreaming" or Creation, to help memorize the way and so "learn the country".

To most tourists Uluru – or Ayers Rock (as it was named by explorer William Gosse in 1873 to honour his benefactor) – is still a climb to be conquered or a radiant landmark to be photographed en masse from the Sunset Viewing Area. But a far better way of getting into the spirit of the place is to take the nine-kilometre walk through waist-high grass around its base. Geologically the massif is a series of near-vertical strata inexplicably thrust up above all around it. Looking rather like a weathered loaf of sliced bread, its grooves and cliffs vary with your perspective. Approaching the "slices" end-on reveals smooth gullies carved into the rock and feeding waterholes like Mutijulu Springs shaded by groves of casuarina oaks. A few kilometres further the steep flanks harbour caves and bizarre scalloped formations, some of them sacred sites fenced off from visitors: every bend in the track offers another startling profile. When you're back at the start of the circuit, hot and sticky from the sun, you can be satisfied that you've experienced the Rock and not merely stood on top of it.

need to know

Most people start the 2- to 3-hour walk from the main car park at the base of the climb. **Ayers Rock Resort** (@www.ayersrockresort.com.au) is 15km from Uluru and served by flights from most state capitals. Entry to the park costs Aus$25 and is valid for three days.

6 Meeting the crocs at Shady Camp, NT

Evolving in isolation over millions of years, Australia's idiosyncratic wildlife is the stuff of Disney cartoons. The island continent has given us the bounding kangaroo, the duck-billed platypus (thought to be a hoax when introduced to Victorian society), and who can resist those cuddly koalas? Up in the "Top End" of the country, the shores of the Van Diemen Gulf east of Darwin hold a log-jam of big crocodiles. Though the saltwater or estuarine crocodile is not unique to north Australia, the size they can reach here is exceptional: the biggest examples of the world's largest reptiles.

Croc farms around the country allow you to safely poke fun at these gnarled primeval beasts; many favourites are huge, battle-scarred "rogue crocs" brought into captivity after menacing some remote community. But take away the fencing and a one-to-one wild encounter with the jagged Silurian scowl of a mature saltie will send a quiver of fascinated revulsion across your skin. You won't get that kind of frisson from a koala's grin!

The best place for a guaranteed fence-free encounter is the tidal barrage at Shady Camp, an old buffalo-hunting base on the Mary River, north of the Arnhem Highway. Here the ebb and flow of the rich tropical sludge gives the resident reptiles all the sustenance they need: fat barramundi or catfish; gangly storks or ibis – sometimes snatched from the air; and feral water buffalo trapped in monsoonal mud. The menu even includes fellow crocs and, of course, you and me.

Territory lore is full of tales of menacing croc attacks and now, nearly half a century after commercial hunting was banned, those Sixties baby-boomers are reaching maturity of eight metres or more and a ton in weight. As you putter among the Shady Camp lilies in your rented outboard, just inches above the occluded surface, sun-baking salties open one eye, slide down the muddy banks and disappear into the water: a timid or provocative response? Hopefully you'll never find out.

need to know

Shady Camp is 200km east of Darwin (last 60km is 2WD dirt road). Some Kakadu tours include an excursion here but you can easily rent a boat nearby from Aus$70 for 2 hours including fuel (☎08/8978 8937). Croc sightings are guaranteed anytime.

Watching footy at the MCG

A Saturday "arvo" at the Melbourne Cricket Ground reveals Melbourne at its best. All ages, races and classes are united by one passion: Australian Rules, or "footy" as it's known in this sports-mad city. Footy is Melbourne's religion, and the locals have been passionate followers since the 1850s, when it was first invented here to keep cricketers fit in winter.

Each match attracts tens of thousands of fans, and despite a move to a national competition (much to the despair of some Melbournians, who saw their teams fold or merge as a result), Melbourne remains at the heart of the game, with its temple the MCG, known as "the G", located a short stroll from the city centre.

Every weekend the nearby railway stations and roads are clogged with fans heading in to "barrack" for their team. If you plan to see a game, choose one between traditional rivals such as Essendon and Carlton, two of Melbourne's oldest teams; the atmosphere will be electric with a guaranteed full house, split 50/50. Tense but never violent, rowdy but not without humour, you'll see just as many women as men cheering on their team.

Footy is a physical game without the ferocity of rugby or the theatrics of soccer. The players are usually tall and lean, as the game requires strength, athleticism and endurance. It includes kicking, catching, handpasses, footpasses, tackles, bounces, bumps and no offside rule. The players have been known to run up to twenty kilometres in a match lasting 120 minutes and divided into quarters.

In the stalls big men wave pompoms in team colours. The fun begins with rousing traditional team songs as players run onto the field, breaking through huge crepe-paper banners. A catch is called a "mark", a spectacular mark is a "speccie" and the umpires are derogatorily referred to as "white maggots".

Still confused? Any fan sitting next to you will be happy to fill you in on the finer points. Should you choose to support their team, you're likely to gain a lifelong mate. After all, nothing makes a devotee of a religion happier than a successful conversion.

need to know

The footy season runs from late March to the last Saturday in September. Admission to the MCG is around Aus$20.

21

RIVER DEEP MOUNTAIN HIGH: Bushwalking the Overland track

need to know

Most walkers tackle the track from north to south to get the potentially bad weather behind them; it's the mandatory direction between November and April. There are six basic unattended cabins along the way, available on a first come first served basis, or you can carry a tent.

Entry to the park requires a permit plus Aus$100 registration fee.

See @www.overlandtrack.com.au. In summer daily buses from Hobart, Queenstown, Launceston and Devonport serve each end of the walk.

Australia's best-known long-distance bushwalk leads from Tasmania's highest peak to Australia's deepest lake across a magnificent alpine wilderness, unbroken by roads and adorned by brooding lakes, glacier-carved cirques and thundering waterfalls.

Stormy skies are frequent on Tassie, but even on the ground there's no shortage of drama with features named after their classical Greek counterparts – Mount Eros, the Acropolis, and Lake Elysia – providing a fitting backdrop to the Olympian landscape. And though much of the 65-kilometre trail is boardwalk with bridged creeks, there's no escaping several muddy interludes – be prepared to get wet.

This is Tasmania, so fresh drinking water is plentiful and need not be carried; the daunting task is lugging enough food and stove fuel for the duration. Once you accept that, the exhilaration of wandering completely self-sufficient through the mountain wilderness fills you with a sense of deep satisfaction. Up above, currawongs and eagles cut through the skies, while below you quolls and wallabies abound.

It takes about a week to tramp across the Overland's stirring range of landscapes, though you'll want to add a day or two for side trips to waterfalls, lakes and scrambling up peaks such as Mount Ossa, Tasmania's highest at 1617m, overlooking forests of King Billy pines and carpeted in fragrant wildflowers in early summer. Even then you're sure to have rain and even snow at some point, and eventually you'll stagger aboard the Lake St Clair ferry, aching, mud-caked but happy, for an uncelebrated return to civilization.

THE BAROSSA

While it's still said that "real men drink beer", nowadays many a true-blue Aussie bloke can tell his Shiraz from his Cabernet, his Semillon from his Riesling. And a wine-tasting weekend is now as much part of the Australian lifestyle as a barbecue in the backyard.

By far the best-known wine region in Australia is the Barossa Valley, an hour's drive northeast of Adelaide; it is also one of Australia's oldest – some of the vines planted over 150 years ago still bear fruit today. The valley's Mediterranean climate and soil are perfect for producing full-bodied reds and robust whites. Almost every Barossa winery has a Shiraz or Shiraz blend on their books – strong, dark wines with a full-fruited aroma and a round, velvety structure, while Riesling is the staple among the Barossa whites, rounded and full-flavoured with passionfruit and lime aromas.

The Winemaker Trail takes you through Barossa's picturesque hamlets and across rolling hills to its sixty wineries, many of which offer tastings and cellar door sales. Among the big-name establishments, Wolf Blass and Jacob's Creek are perennially popular, but also worth checking out is Bethany Wines, run by the same family for six generations, and up-and-coming Two Hands.

For the novice, wine-tasting can be a daunting experience. Try the wine in the order suggested by the winery, moving from whites and sparkling to reds, following the **five S's of wine-tasting**: **See** (study the colour); **Swirl** (allows the wine to breathe); **Sniff** (our sense of smell is more acute than our

sense of taste); **Sip**; **Savour** (swirl around in the mouth to appreciate the flavour). Swallowing is optional; if you're visiting a lot of wineries it's probably better to spit out. Chances are you will walk away with a few bottles of your favourite — and a brand new vocabulary to boot.

need to know

Numerous day tours operate out of Adelaide, ranging from personalized limousine services to backpacker tours in a minivan. With more time on your hands you could stay in the valley and hire a bike to get around. Pick up a copy of the Winemaker Trail map from the Barossa Wine and Information Centre in Tanunda.

Ⓦwww.southaustralia.com
Ⓦwww.wineaustralia.com
Ⓦwww.jacobscreek.com
Ⓦwww.peterlehmannwines.com
Ⓦwww.bethany.com.au
Ⓦwww.twohandswines.com

Slip into Broometime

The laid-back, romantic appeal of Broome stems partly from its uniqueness along the west Australian coastline.

need to know

There are frequent flights to Broome from Perth and other state capitals, plus packages offering a wide choice of accommodation from hostels to exclusive resorts. See also @www. broomevisitorcentre.com.au.

In many thousands of kilometres no other town matches its alluring combination of beautiful beaches and relative sophistication. Grotty, industrial Port Hedland, the next town, is 600km and many more light years away.

From its earliest days, Broome's had an ethnically diverse population: Timorese, Malays and Chinese came in their thousands to get rich quick when the pearl industry boomed here in the late 1800s. The world's largest oysters prospered in the tidal waters and shells were originally shovelled off the beach. With the invention of the diving helmet, Asian divers kept the supply going, but along with frequent cyclones the new-fangled technology caused many deaths, as a stroll around the town's different ethnic cemeteries reveals. Pearl farming continues today offshore, from securely guarded pontoons, and Broome remains the best place to buy these gems, particularly along Dampier Terrace.

The old Chinatown has been tastefully renovated, its once grubby tin-shack bordellos are now trendy boutiques, while a mile away the former master pearlers' bougainvillea-shrouded villas house galleries and coffee shops. Nearby, the 1916 Broome Picture House, the world's oldest open-air cinema, predating Hollywood, is still going strong. Bats flutter across the latest release on screen as you watch under starlight from communal canvas benches; the new air-con cinema round the corner just misses the point.

Nature has further blessed Broome with heavenly Cable Beach; here a contented indolence permeates your bones as palm fronds waft lazily in the breeze. The classic vista from Gantheaume Point lays red cliffs over ivory sands and a sea so hypnotically turquoise it should carry a health warning. A few years ago some bright spark cooked up the "Stairway to the Moon", the occasional "staircase" illusion created by the moon rising over the low-tide mudflats when viewed from Town Beach. It sounds better than it looks but you don't mind, you're on Broometime after all.

SYDNEY HARBOUR-MASTERING

The urge to emigrate always surfaces when you take the public ferry across Sydney Harbour: for the views from the deck not only encompass the city's two biggest icons – the Sydney Harbour Bridge and the Sydney Opera House – but also the stuff of daily Sydney life. Who wouldn't want to live in a harbour-view apartment, drop by one of the countless sandy beaches on the way home from work, learn to sail? And to cap it all, you could be taking this ferry on your daily commute from downtown Sydney to a home in Manly, 12km north, a suburb which has not one but two beaches of its own, one facing the harbour, the other overlooking the high-rolling surf of the Pacific Ocean.

Fittingly, the Manly ferry sets off from alongside Sydney's oldest neighbourhood, The Rocks, site of the first permanent European settlement in 1788, and now a sort of neighbourhood theme park, with its preserved homes, museums and twee cafés. A few minutes later it chugs

you within waving distance of the Bridge before all eyes swivel right for captivating views of the shell-shaped Opera House, at its most dazzling like this, with sea-sparkle in the foreground.

Need a different perspective? Then sign up for the Bridge Climb, a three-and-a-half-hour tour that takes you on to the girders of Sydney Harbour Bridge itself, and up to the summit of its eastern arch, 134m above the harbour waters. Once primed and prepped, you're clad in a regulation steel-grey jumpsuit and clipped on, steeplejack-style, to the railings, as you negotiate ladders and catwalks in the footsteps of your tour leader. Aside from awesome high-level vistas, you get to learn about the construction of its mammoth 503-metre-long arch, completed in 1932. Seventy-five years on and the Harbour Bridge is still the enduring symbol of the Sydney good life, linking the city's energetic business and historical districts with those ever-so-desirable North Shore suburbs across the water.

need to know

Ferries to Manly depart about every half-hour until 11.45pm and take 30 minutes. **The Bridge Climb** operates daily (prices, which vary according to time of day and the season, range from Aus$169 to Aus$295; (ⓦwww.bridgeclimb.com).

12 CANYONEERING IN KARJINI, WA

Listed as one of "100 Things A Man Must Do In His Life" by FHM magazine, canyoneering through Karijini National Park is an Indiana Jones-style adventure through a rarely seen wonderland of towering red rock canyons, trickling waterfalls and hidden pools. Be prepared for half a day of walking then crawling, wading then swimming, climbing along ledges and up waterfalls and then jumping into freezing pools.

Part of the experience includes Knox Gorge; descending the steep track into the ravine you've little idea of what waits ahead. Paths and ledges peter out and you're forced to swim across a couple of pools until the walls narrow suddenly into a shoulder-wide slot that never sees direct sunlight. You enter the chasm, bridging over jammed boulders, deafened and disoriented by water running through your legs until it seems there is no way ahead. There is, but to continue you must hurtle blindly down the "do-or-die" Knox Slide into an unseen plunge pool below. Amazed that you've survived that, you now make a six-metre jump or abseil off the next waterfall to emerge into the broad sunlit waters of Red Gorge, the park's main canyon.

From here you swim, wade and scramble over the debris washed down by the last cyclone until you reach the Four Gorges area. Hundreds of feet above, tourists at Oxer's Lookout point and stare, wondering how on earth you got there. Meanwhile, you're wondering how you're going to get out. The secret is to ascend the stepped ledges alongside Weano Falls and follow the canyon upstream until you emerge at Handrail Pool in the regular tourist zone. Once you're out, all that remains is to stagger over to Oxer's Lookout yourself and peer down in amazement at what you've just achieved.

NEED TO KNOW

Karijini National Park is 1400km northeast of Perth. It's strongly advised to only explore the inner gorges with a responsible guide, usually as part of a multi-day tour from Perth or Port Hedland.

13

learning to surf on the

GOLD
COAST

Mastering the art of riding a wave is not as tricky as it looks, and the southernmost coast of Queensland is one of the best surfing nurseries on the planet.

Here the swell along the 40km beach from Coolangatta to South Stradbroke Island is untamed by the Barrier Reef's wave-dampening atolls further north. Between those two points you can't miss the high-rise blight of Surfers Paradise, Australia's domestic holidaymaking "Costa", but as far as you're concerned it's the reliable and easy surf that matters.

With tropical cyclones animating the Pacific swell, summer is the time to watch the surfing pros, while the temperate winter is the time to learn. From April to October the regular waves break safely over sand here and the warm, waist-deep water makes it all the more pleasurable. If you've got a good sense of balance, you'll be at an advantage; though most surf schools promise to have you at least standing on the board by the end of a typical two-hour session, and surfing properly in a day or two.

Catching a wave is the name of the game, something that you can teach yourself anytime on a short boogie board. The next big step on a full-size board is getting from prone to on your feet and arms out. Soon enough you'll be moving over the water and adopting the classic stance, even if the wave's only halfway up your shin. Get it right and you'll experience a taste of the bigger rush, the raw surge of adrenaline which is what surfing's all about. But everyone's got to start somewhere and for the novice surf junkie the beaches around Surfers Paradise couldn't be more aptly named.

need to know

Beginners pay around Aus$50 for a two-hour session. Try **Surfers Paradise Free Ride Surfing School** (ⓦwww.freeridesurfing.com.au), **Cheyne Horan School of Surf** (ⓦwww.cheynehoran.com.au) or **Australian Surfer** (ⓦwww.australiansurfer.com). You can rent a board from Aus$25 a day.

14
getting to grips with

Aboriginal art in Alice Springs

There's no need for in-flight entertainment when you're flying across Australia because the view from the plane is always arresting. The endless, barely inhabited Outback looks spectacular from the air, a vast natural canvas of ivory-coloured salt pans, clumps of grey-green scrub, and sienna, ochre and russet sands, scored by the occasional dead-straight line of an oil exploration track or the wiggle of a long-dried watercourse. It's like one enormous abstract picture and, in part at least, that's what informs many Aboriginal artworks, particularly the so-called dot paintings.

At the heart of many Aboriginal traditions are practices for surviving in the extreme conditions of Outback Australia and the need to pass on this knowledge to descendants. Historically, one way of doing that has been to draw a map in the dust, detailing crucial local features such as sacred landmarks, waterholes and food sources. These sand paintings are elaborate and take days to create; they are also sacred and to be viewed only by initiated clan members before being destroyed. But in the early 1970s, a teacher at Papunya, northwest of Alice Springs, began encouraging young Aborigine kids to translate their sand-painting techniques on to canvas. In fact it was the elders who took to the idea – without divulging culturally secret information, of course – and a new art form was born.

Those early Papunya artists have been superseded by painters from throughout the central desert, the most successful experimenting with innovative abstract and minimalist styles in their bid to woo international collectors. Alice Springs now has two dozen art galleries devoted to Aboriginal art, with paintings priced between Aus$40 and Aus$40,000. Browsing these galleries is one of the highlights of a visit to Alice and even if you don't bring a picture home, you'll come away with a different perspective on the Outback.

need to know

Recommended Aboriginal-owned galleries in Alice Springs include **Papunya Tula Artists** (🌐www.papunyatula.com.au) as well as the **Desart** artists' co-operative (🌐www.desart.com.au).

ROAD TRIP DOWN UNDER

PERTH TO DARWIN TO ADELAIDE

15

WHO CAN RESIST THE APPEAL OF THE OPEN ROAD?

The lonesome highway, good company, and your favourite track on the stereo. Allowing hostel happy-hours to merge into weeks or getting lobstered under the ozone hole is all very well, but it's a big country out there, one which is full of adventure.

Let's say you settle for an easy-going two-month trip of around 8000km, from Perth to Darwin and down to Adelaide. Once out of the city you can count the number of traffic lights all the way to Adelaide on the fingers of one hand. It's the open road all right; any more open and you'd fall right through it.

Don't expect too much until you can get past Kalbarri or even Monkey Mia, 1000km from Perth. Near here you cross the 26th parallel and a sign proclaims: "Welcome to the Nor'West"; now you're in the real Outback. Be warned: from now on you need to fill up your tank at every roadhouse, and you may end up camping in lay-bys, so be prepared; it's all part of the adventure.

North of Carnarvon, lovely Coral Bay is worth the diversion, as is swinging inland to explore the awesome gorges in Karijini National Park. Chilling in laid-back Broome is compulsory, too, before heading across the top to Northern Territory's capital, Darwin, still 2000km away and nearer to Singapore than Sydney. Whatever the season, wet or dry, it's hot here, day and night.

From Darwin you head south down the barrel of the 3000km Stuart Highway. Triple-trailer roadtrains almost blow you off the road and the stark, dusty landscape makes you ponder, "just how many anthills are there in the Northern Territory?" As you near the Central Desert, crisp horizons stretch out. The air feels fresher, the locals less deranged. You don't want to miss seeing Uluru or a night spent underground in the opal-mining town of Coober Pedy. Then Adelaide, and right on cue your long-suffering wagon's doors fall off. Patch it up and sell it on. It did it once and it can do it again.

16

Indulge your tastebuds
at Queen Victoria Market, Melbourne

A visit to Queen Victoria Market, or "Vic Market", located on the northern fringe of the city centre, is a superb introduction to Melbourne's vibrant food culture and will have you rubbing shoulders with everyone from government ministers to the city's best chefs. Running for 128 years, it's one of the oldest markets in Australia, and is liveliest on the weekends when buskers compete with spruiking stallholders for your attention.

For foodies there are three main areas: the Deli section, the Meat and Fish Hall, and the fruit and vegetable market. The Deli is characterized by its strong smells and its shops selling regional specialities such as fine local cheeses, including the Jindi Triple Cream Brie and Milawa's tasty goat varieties, as well as lesser-known fusions like kangaroo biltong (South African-style dried meat). Arriving hungry you'll find the free tastings will put a stop to the pangs as quickly as they tempt you to lighten your wallet. Greek, Italian, French and Polish stalls stock everything from marinated octopus to juniper sausage, while speciality butchers sell emu and crocodile, in addition to the usual quail, rabbit and venison. If you're looking for more traditional meat offerings, head to the Meat and Fish Hall. Here, competition is fierce, with dozens of butchers supplying prime cuts of meat from a leg of lamb to Japanese-style Wagu beef, and fishmongers stalls groan under an impressive display of fish and shellfish on ice, including northern Australian wild Barramundi, Victorian crayfish and fresh Tasmanian oysters.

The fruit and vegetable market reflects the seasons, dominated by root vegetables in winter and stone fruits in summer – the proximity of Southeast Asia means exotic fruits like mangosteens, rambutan and the pungent-smelling durian are also available.

If you're after something less epicurean, however, try the German Bratwurst shop for a sauerkraut and mustard covered sausage, or the American Doughnut Van, serving up bags of jam-filled doughnuts.

Vic Market is a fantastic way to experience the many cultures that make Melbourne what it is today – and to get a taste for where it's going.

QUEEN VICTORIA MARKET

LANDJAGER
$5 A PAIR
VERY TASTY

DOUGHNUTS

ughnut Kitchen

TOPUS 699 kg

BA
SA

need to know
Food Market opens 6am–2pm (closed Mon & Wed).
Foodie Tours (@www.qvm.com.au)
available 10–noon on market days costing from
Aus$28 (☎03/9320 5835).

sea kayaking
around
Shark Bay, WA

The Peron Peninsula in Shark Bay, on the north-west coast of Western Australia, is well known for its regular dolphin visitations, and a beachside resort at Monkey Mia has grown around the spectacle.

But there's much more to this UNESCO-listed reserve than meeting Flipper and the family, and the sheltered conditions make the Shark Bay area ideal for a sea kayaking adventure.

Paddling in a bay named after the ocean's deadliest predator may sound as sensible as skinny-dipping in Piranha Creek. Sure, there are tiger sharks out in the depths, but the abundant sea life means they're fed well enough not to bother you in the shallows. Besides the pleasures of gliding serenely across bottle-green waters and camping beneath paprika-red cliffs on whichever deserted beach takes your fancy, marine-life spotting adds a "sea safari" element to your trip. Don't be surprised if before long a green turtle passes under your kayak, followed by rays the size of a tablecloth. And where there are rays there are usually sharks, but only frisky babies less than a metre long, maturing in the shallow nurseries before heading out to sea.

Battling the winds around Cape Peron there's a good chance you'll encounter dugongs grazing in the sea grass meadows, and as you cruise down the sheltered side of the peninsula flocks of cormorants, terns and pelicans will take to the air. Finally, if you've not seen any already, bottlenosed dolphins are a guaranteed sight at Monkey Mia, which is also a great place for a day paddle.

need to know

Denham (900km north of Perth) is a good place to put in for a typical five-day, 100km trip. Bring your own kayak; or hire one from Denham and **Monkey Mia Vistor Centre** (29 Knight Terrace ☎1300/135887), carry enough water and inform the ranger in Denham (☎08/9948 1208) of your itinerary. Aim for early morning starts before the southwesterlies set in, and mid-afternoon beach camps to enjoy the remains of the day.

18
buzzing over the Bungles

If you've never been in a helicopter then a flight over Purnululu National Park – or the Bungle Bungles as most people call it – makes a great initiation. This mass of orange and black striped beehive-like domes is amazing enough at ground level, but leaning out of the doorless cockpit, your foot on the landing rail, you'll have a grin as wide as the Fitzroy River as you swoop and soar over the maze of 200-metre-deep chasms between the "bungles". At one point you launch low off the plateau and in an instant the ground disappears, sending your stomach spiralling.

Each dome ranges from 10 to 40 metres high but altogether cover just a small part of the park's 25,000 square kilometres of lightly wooded hills and grassland. To local Aboriginal people Purnululu has been a sacred site for millennia, but the wonders of this remote region of north-western Australia were only fully acknowledged in the 1980s when a TV crew came across it while filming a documentary about over-grazing. Recognizing these curious rock formations to be geologically unique, Purnululu National Park was created in 1987, with access purposely limited to small aircraft or high-clearance vehicles able to negotiate the twisting 53km access track.

The origin of the domes is still unclear. The theory of a meteor impact shattering the rock into the now weathered segments takes a knock when one sees mini-bungle formations elsewhere in the Kimberley. More mundane, but more likely, it's a result of deposition, uplifting and subsequent erosion. The banding, on the other hand, is a clear illustration of eons of alternating sediments: the orange deposits (iron oxide) are not porous while the rock above and below holds water and supports the growth of black lichen, which forms a fragile crust.

And "fragile" may well describe your knees as you climb out of the helicopter and wobble across the launch pad. Now you've seen them from the air it's time for a closer inspection on foot.

need to know

The park is 110km north of Halls Creek (allow 3 hours) and is open from April to December, weather permitting. Entry is Aus$9 per day per car. Without your own 4WD, take a two- or three-day tour from Kununurra, 250km to the northwest, from Aus$299. Flights can be booked at the park's airstrip and cost from Aus$200 for 30 minutes.

19
RIVER OF
NO RETURN:
RAFTING the FRANKLIN

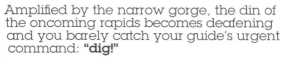

Amplified by the narrow gorge, the din of the oncoming rapids becomes deafening and you barely catch your guide's urgent command: **"dig!"**

You claw at the water with your paddle and hurtle towards the abyss. With your eyes tight shut the raft tips over the brink and is all but lost amid the spray, screams and flailing limbs. It's yet another miraculous escape on Tasmania's white-water rollercoaster but already you want more.

Most of the Franklin-Gordon Wild Rivers National Park – part of the 1.4 million hectare Tasmanian Wilderness World Heritage Area – is an inaccessible mass of ravines cloaked in temperate rainforest so, short of reincarnating as a parrot, the only way to experience this pristine wilderness is astride a raft. You're probably only going to be here once so go for the full monty: a 120-kilometre, ten-day expedition from the Lyell Highway to the coastal town of Strahan.

The great thing about rafting is its excellent thrill-to-safety ratio. Stuffed into a wetsuit, life jacket and helmet, you'll feel comfortingly invulnerable. Which is just as well, as once in there's no way out for days at a time, though this daunting isolation is also part of the appeal. By day two you'll be locked inside the Franklin's tortured quartzite gorges, and that's how things stay for the rest of the tour, while you negotiate the all-too-aptly named Cauldron and Thunderush rapids, and the suitably messy Pig Trough.

Most nights you'll camp where you can, squeezed onto any available level patch of the riverbank, so be ready to rough it. Your guide will know which rapids are best portaged round depending on the water level: the Franklin's catchment is so vast, a storm blowing in off the Southern Ocean can raise levels twenty feet in a matter of hours.

On reaching the Gordon River the pace slows to a gentle descent and it all ends with a dramatic flight to Strahan in a seaplane or a more sedate trip aboard a yacht.

need to know

A ten-day expedition with **Water By Nature** (🌐www.franklinrivertasmania.com), **Rafting Tasmania** (🌐www.raftingtasmania.com) or **Tasmanian Expeditions** (🌐www.tas-ex.com) costs around Aus$2300.

FOUR-WHEELING
through croc country:
Cairns to Cape York

Most of us have little use for 4WDs but in a particular corner of Australia these all-terrain machines can provide the sort of adventure they were truly built for. Cape York, Australia's northernmost point, is over a 1000km from Cairns, with challenging driving that will demand concentration and an understanding of your vehicle's abilities as you gingerly inch across tidal creeks inhabited by crocodiles.

From Cairns head out along the scenic Captain Cook Highway to Cooktown: the last settlement of any size on your "Trip to the Tip". Choose either the coastal route via Cape Tribulation, where Cook's *Endeavour* nearly sank in 1770 or, for a real adventure, the infamous "CREB Track" out of Daintree. Here's your chance to play with the transfer levers as you run along the CREB's tyre-clawing gradients to the Lion's Den Hotel, a classic "bush pub" dating back to 1875.

Past Cooktown the Lakefield National Park is Queensland's answer to Kakadu, with "magnetic" anthills aligned north–south to avoid overheating in the noonday sun, 180 species of birds and a rich colony of flying foxes.

But there's more. A tough, creek-ridden diversion leads east to the Iron Range National Park, where the creeper-festooned rainforests don't recede until Chilli Beach campsite on the Coral Sea. Ecologically this extraordinary park has more in common with New Guinea and is famed for the nocturnal green python and brilliant blue-and-red eclectus parrot.

Back on the main road die-hards avoid the newer bypasses to follow the Old Telegraph Track's numerous creek crossings. Eventually you arrive at Twin Falls, with its safe swimming holes, before reaching the 100-metre-wide Jardine River, a once demanding crossing now made easier by the nearby ferry. Then suddenly the road runs out near a rocky headland overlooking the Torres Straits. A sign marks the tip of mainland Australia and the end of your journey.

need to know
Renting a fully equipped 4WD "bush-camper" in Cairns costs from Aus$220 a day; allow at least a fortnight for the return trip. Travel is only possible out of wet season from May to November.

21 swimming with
Whale Sharks
at Ningaloo

Once a year the world's largest fish makes an appearance at the Ningaloo Reef fringing Western Australia's North West Cape.

Its arrival is strategically timed with a moonlit night in late summer when coral polyps spawn en masse, ejecting millions of eggs into the tropical waters. Guided by some arcane instinct on their northbound migration from the polar depths, the hungry whale sharks are waiting, mouths agape.

More whale than shark, this fifteen-metre-long gentle giant is twice the size of the great white of Jaws fame but entirely harmless to humans. It survives by ingesting all the krill, plankton and seasonal spawn that its metre-wide mouth can scoop in. For the whale shark the weeks that follow the coral spawning are equivalent to being locked up in a sweetshop for a night.

Not surprisingly the North West Cape has become the world's prime destination for diving and snorkelling with these seasonal stars of Ningaloo. Spotter planes search for the telltale shadows and radio the boats below, which race into position ahead of the shark: after what may have been many hours of waiting, suddenly it's all action as you hurriedly don your kit. On the boat's rear platform they give the signal and you leap in, fins kicking hard, following the lead diver. As the bubbles clear a solitary grey silhouette looms out of the murk, its back speckled with white spots. With lazy sweeps of its tailfin, this oceanic behemoth glides gently by and for a couple of minutes, using your own fins, you do your best to keep up. This silent encounter with a shark longer than the boat you just jumped off should trigger alarm bells but strangely, as you swim alongside, you're mesmerized by its benign bulk until it dives effortlessly down into the abyss. You rise to the surface elated at having crossed paths with the biggest shark on the planet – and lived to tell the tale.

need to know
There are daily flights (@www.skywest.com.au) from Perth to the small town of Exmouth on the North West Cape. The best time to see whale sharks is between April and July. A typical day with the sharks costs from Aus$330 including gear and lunch. Licensed operators include **Three Islands** (@www.whalesharkdive.com) and **Exmouth Diving Centre** @www.exmouthdiving.com).

22 STATIONED AT THE LAST FRONTIER: WORKING ON A CATTLE STATION

Working on a Kimberley cattle station will be "hard yakka" as they say out here: hard graft for long hours and low pay. You'll be sharing a bunkhouse and meals with rangy stockmen, and objects like TV, telephones, the Internet and even the radio are luxuries you'll have learn to live without.

But when it's over and the aches have subsided, you'll look back with satisfaction. Instead of passively consuming you'll have participated in an iconic Australian activity immortalized in books like Mary Durack's *Kings in Grass Castles*. You'll have learnt how to brand a bull, built up plenty of muscle, and experienced life in the fabled "Nor'west".

The Kimberley is Australia's last frontier, a place where cattle stations run to a million acres and are on the margins of manageability. The rugged landscape and climate (which in turn floods then burns) make this the harshest cattle country in Australia. But eager hands are always sought so you'll be welcomed, particularly if you've an aptitude for working with horses or motorbikes. With a bit of luck you'll be part of the annual muster, when cattle are tracked down and driven in from the four corners of the property for transport to market. Most stations use horses, dirt- and quad bikes for this, all coordinated from above by helicopters equipped with radios, but you'll be just as useful on foot, coaxing the nervy beasts into mobile yards or triple-trailer roadtrains. You may even get a ride in a bull-catcher, a stripped-down jeep that literally chases, knocks down and half parks on top of the biggest bulls so you can rope them up and drag them into the trailers.

As the theme song of the famous TV show Rawhide put it:

"DON'T TRY TO UNDERSTAND 'EM. JUST ROPE, THROW, AND BRAND 'EM. SOON WE'LL BE LIVING HIGH AND WIDE. RAWHIDE!"

NEED TO KNOW
A typical job last three months and pays Aus$400 a week; see @www.visitoz.org for more details.

2

Visit Adelaide,
the City of Festivals

The Adelaide Festival of Arts is the big one, established in 1960 by a forward-thinking journalist who hoped to replicate Scotland's Edinburgh Festival Downunder. Today it attracts a diverse range of international and Australian performers, with free concerts and open-air film performances, and energizes the city from late February to mid-March every even-numbered year.

A lively avant-garde Fringe festival parallels this event, and recently the Adelaide Film Festival has joined in too, premiering Rolf De Heer's *Ten Canoes*, the first Australian feature to be filmed in an indigenous language. There's even an Adelaide Festival of Ideas held every July in odd years, addressing prescient economic, cultural and environmental issues.

The Fringe kicks off with a street parade down Rundle Street followed by music and comedy at venues around town, all oiled by the 24-hour licensing laws. Previous artists have included Inga Liljeström, described as "Björk, Portishead and Marianne Faithfull on the set of a David Lynch film", and the Musafir Gypsies of Rajasthan, whose music fuses with acrobatics and magic in the tradition of ancient desert wanderers. Jazz trumpeter Vince Jones has also performed, as well as the Pat Metheny Trio and the Amsterdam Sinfonietta, playing Shostakovich and Mozart. Theatre may range from a groundbreaking "shoe opera" about Imelda Marcos, Shakespeare and Ibsen to an adaptation of Peter Goldsworthy's black comedy, *Honk If You Are Jesus*.

Still uninspired? Then perhaps the annual Womadelaide music weekend held in early March in the Botanic Park is for you. Attracting over 70,000 visitors, it's a great place to encounter home-grown talent as well as international artists such as Baaba Maal, the Abdullah Ibrahim Trio and Gilberto Gil. Recently the Saltwater Band from Arnhemland performed alongside reggae journeyman Jimmy Cliff and Miriam Makeba. In short, if you can't find something to stimulate your interest in Adelaide

need to know
Full details on the web at
Ⓦwww.adelaidefestival.org.au,
Ⓦwww.adelaidefringe.com.au,
Ⓦwww.adelaidefilmfestival.org,
Ⓦwww.womadelaide.com.au

ISLAND DREAMING
Sailing the Whitsundays

There's a distinct feeling of déja-vu cruising in a sailboat among the Whitsunday Islands.

Presently it comes to you: you've been here many times, in your lottery fantasies. This tropical idyll of turquoise seas lapping ivory sands against a backdrop of dense green foliage is ingrained in our imagination, be it some Jungian folk memory or saturation advertising. The Beach before it all turned sour. **Paradise.**

Just over 1200km north of Brisbane, this compact archipelago of 70-odd islands lies just off Airlie Beach, a young-at-heart resort described by locals as "a drinking town with a sailing problem". Out at sea you have a delectable menu of islands to choose from: Hayman, which offers resorts so posh staff scurry unseen along tunnels; others like Long Island are more affordable; or you might prefer the Molle Islands, home to little more than a couple of basic campsites. Most are uninhabited.

Sheltered by the **Great Barrier Reef**, the Pacific swell is dampened, but reliable light breezes remain, making the Whitsundays a sailing haven, and at an affordable price. Choose between a sedate three-day cruise, where you can laze aboard a spacious and comfortable crewed boat, or get stuck in and crew on a huge racing "maxi yacht" catering for partying backpackers.

Either way life becomes sybaritically simple. By day you commune with turtles, dolphins and even whales – up from the Antarctic to give birth before heading south again. Or go snorkelling on the lookout for morays and parrotfish (the northeastern tip of Hook Island is best). Come sunset you moor in one of the many unnamed bays while the chef prepares a fresh seafood meal. A shower is as simple as diving into the surrounding water, and your bed is the deck of the boat or the sand on the beach.

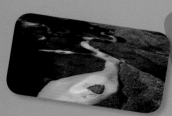

need to know
A two-night, three-day outing from Airlie Beach costs Aus$350–480. Contact **Aussie Adventure Sailing** (@www.aussiesailing.com.au) for excursions on classic tall ships for up to 21 passengers; or **Southern Cross** (@www.soxsail.com.au), which offers tours on maxi-yacht racers, including a high-speed, 21-metre-long America's Cup challenger accommodating 14 passengers, usually couples.

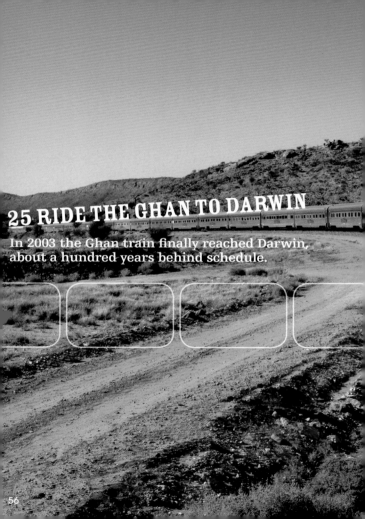

25 RIDE THE GHAN TO DARWIN

In 2003 the Ghan train finally reached Darwin,
about a hundred years behind schedule.

Constructing a reliable rail link between these two towns took up most of the last century but around the millennium the government decided to plug the 1500-kilometre gap from Alice to Darwin and so a legendary transcontinental railway journey was completed.

For most of the two-day northbound ride the train passes through uninhabited Outback, far from the highway and sporadic settlements. Just a couple of hours out of Adelaide and you're already lost on the vast Nullarbor Plain. Night falls and bleached saltpans glow eerily in the moonlight as you tuck yourself in to your comfy four-berth cabin. Next morning the view from the dining car reveals classic Outback colours: clear blue skies, grey-green scrub and rich orange sand. While you stare, doze or read the train passes close to the geographical centre of the continent, and by lunchtime squeezes through the West MacDonnell Ranges into the likeable desert town of Alice Springs for a couple of hours' break.

Past Alice, the Ghan works its way through the ranges before spilling out onto the featureless 1000-kilometre Tanami Desert. The sun sets as you near Wycliffe Well roadhouse, famous for its UFO sightings. You peer keenly into the blackness but see only your reflection and so turn in. Dawn delivers you to the tropical Top End. Trees have reappeared for the first time since Adelaide, here interspersed with countless two-metre-high termite mounds. The town of Katherine marks another first on this epic journey – the only flowing river for over 2000km – and then it's just an hour or two to journey's end in Darwin.

Sure, you could've flown here in a few hours, or driven and arrived feeling like week-old roadkill. But by rolling into town on the Ghan your carbon footprint is the size of a possum's front paw. And that is something to feel good about.

need to know

The Ghan leaves Adelaide for Darwin every Friday and Sunday at 5.15pm and takes 48 hours. Seats cost Aus$555, berths Aus$1490 (Wwww.gsr.com.au).

25

Ultimate
experiences
Australia
miscellany

1 Natural attractions

▶▶ Most visited natural attraction

- Kangaroo Island (South Australia)
- Blue Mountains (New South Wales)
- Wilsons Promontory (Victoria)
- Great Barrier Reef (Queensland)
- Lake St Clair (Tasmania)
- The Pinnacles (Western Australia)
- Uluru (Northern Territory)

2 Tucker

The further removed from its Anglo roots, the better Australian cuisine gets. Being its closest neighbour, the rich diversity of **Southeast Asian** cuisine tops the bill for many. One of the best places to try the different flavours and dishes is Darwin at the Thursday night Mindil Beach Sunset Market: the city's strong Asian community is well represented here with nearly sixty food stalls offering an array of sizzlingly fresh fare from over thirty different countries.

▶▶ Five Aussie classics

Pie floater an upside down meat pie, slavered in mushy green peas and tomato sauce.

Chiko Roll a service station and fish 'n' chip shop staple: mutton, cabbage, barley and spices wrapped in thick floury dough, and then deep fried.

Vegemite Australia's equivalent to Marmite, but thicker and stronger tasting.

Lamingtons a square of sponge cake, coated in thick chocolate icing, sugar and coconut.

Pavlova a meringue dessert which is crisp on the outside and soft and gooey in the middle, usually decorated with fresh fruit and cream.

 3 Language

"Strine" (the pronunciation of "Australian" with a very heavy local accent) has its origins in the archaic cockney and Irish of the colony's early convicts as well as the adoption of words from the scores of Aboriginal languages.

4 Outback driving

Driving the Outback highways and even some dirt roads you'll come across the aptly named **roadtrain**, a truck that is towing three and sometimes even four trailers. Commonly used to transport livestock where railways or suitable anchorages do not exist, they're a familiar sight in the northwest of Australia. Overtaking on a sealed road requires a clear long straight but on dirt roads is often impossible as the dust cloud they throw up is up to half a mile long.

Currently the record for the **longest roadtrain** ever assembled stands in Clifton, Queensland. With 104 trailers the train was nearly 1500 metres long and weighed over 1500 tonnes. It was driven over a set distance to claim a Guinness world record in 2006. Preparations are already underway to build a roadtrain over a kilometre long.

5 Books on Australia

▶▶ Five great Australian reads

Dirt Music by Tim Winton. Bleak but beautifully written saga of unravelling west-coast lives.
Songlines by Bruce Chatwin. Absorbing and accessible semi-fictional discourse on the meaning of Aboriginal mythology.
Bliss by Peter Carey. A Sydney executive drops out and heads for a New Age community in rural NSW.
Fatal Shore by Robert Hughes. Minutely detailed account of Australia's colonial origins.
My Place by Sally Morgan. A Western Australian woman discovers her Aboriginal roots.

6 Colonization

Initially no one took much interest in Cook's Antipodean discoveries of 1770, but following American independence from Britain a new penal colony became desperately needed when convicts started clogging up English jails. For seventy years after the First Fleet's arrival in Botany Bay in 1787, 160,000 convicts were transported overseas. Most were poverty-stricken petty thieves and the vast majority served out their sentence to eventually receive a certificate of freedom or ticket of leave. Once free very few ever returned to England.

"Transported 7 years for stealing one pair of shoes"

The Nottingham Quarter Sessions Court passes sentence on labourer Thomas Allsopp on April 10, 1833.

7 People

It is thought the ancestors of today's **Aboriginal people** arrived on the continent via the Indonesian archipelago at least 40,000 years ago, though the date is probably much earlier. This makes today's descendants part of the world's oldest surviving culture.

There were an estimated 750,000 Aboriginal people at the time of colonization in 1787. Following the disastrous impact of this, today's population has recovered to around 450,000 or 2.5 percent of Australia's population.

▶▶ Dreamtime

Aboriginal Dreamtime explains how creative forces shaped the landscape, how humans were created, provides verbal maps of tribal territory and links natural features to the actions of Dreamtime ancestors, who often had both human and animal forms. These stories were often passed down in the form of drawings on the ground or on cave walls, or as dot paintings in the Central and Western deserts.

8 The river wild

Once in a blue moon the Finke River actually flows from its source just west of Alice Springs for 700km all the way to Lake Eyre in South Australia. But the fact that it's been doing it for 400 million years makes many scientists claim it to be the world's oldest river. On the odd occasion a tropical cyclone reaches far enough south to soak the Central Deserts and get the Finke flowing, keen kayakers get twitchy. Leaping into the thick orange current with a few days' supplies, the trick is to get as far downriver as possible before the flash flood peters out.

9 A bed to sleep in

▸▸ Five great hotels

Intercontinental, 117 Macquarie St, Sydney. Get high with stunning harbour views from the top thirty floors of this elegant five-star hotel.

Adelphi Hotel, 187 Flinders Lane, Melbourne. A striking exterior and an ultramodern interior featuring abstract designs make this one of Melbourne's most stylish choices.

Latitude 131°, Ayers Rock Resort, NT. A tucked-away upmarket bush-camp with a handful of luxury tented cabins set among the dunes, all with views of Uluru.

The Bush Camp, Faraway Bay, Kimberley, NT. "You've never been this far away" is the tagline and they're not kidding. Only accessible by small plane or boat, it's a remote coastal wilderness retreat with basic cabins and great food.

Dunk Island Resort, Mission Beach, Qld. Low-key resort on a rainforest-clad humpbacked island 15 minutes by ferry from Mission Beach or an hour's flight from Cairns. Forest walks, snorkelling, heavenly beaches – and it's kid-friendly too.

10 Australiana

Boomerangs are among the most popular souvenirs bought in Australia. Originally used for digging, hunting, fighting and ceremonial purposes, they have actually been found throughout the ancient world. Among those crafted by the Aborigines only some were specifically designed to come back when thrown, most used the same principle as that of today's plane wing to create lift as the flattened stick spun through the air: thousands of years later Leonardo Da Vinci came up with the airfoil theory and a few hundred years after that the Wright Brothers put it into practice. Other popular mementos include stuffed **koalas** and **kangaroos**, **didgeridoos** and Uluru snow-shake **globes**.

11 Religion in Australia

- **Christian** 70.3 percent   (Mostly Catholic and Anglican)
- **Atheist/Agnostic** 16.7   (Includes Humanists and Rationalists)
- **Unknown** 9.8
- **Muslim** 1.1
- **Buddhist** 1.1
- **Jewish** 0.5
- **Hindu** 0.4
- **Sikh** 0.1

12 Highs and lows

Australia is the world's **flattest continent** with only six percent of its land mass rising above 600m. The **highest point** is Mt Kosciuszko in NSW, at just 2228m. The **lowest point** is the usually dry Lake Eyre in South Australia at around 15m below sea level.

 **Sport**

Australians' love of **sport** and **gambling** are closely related though gambling probably came first. The game of **two-up** was brought to Australia by English and Irish convicts and soon spread across the country. It's basically heads or tails but with two coins, thrown up off a wooden "kip". The coins must land as two heads or two tails for the betters of either to win. The greater odds of 4:1 against plain old 2:1 with heads or tails are what gives two-up its edge.

▶▶ Top five sports & main places to watch

Footy (Aussie Rules): MCG, Melbourne

Cricket: SCG Sydney

Rugby League: Suncorp Stadium, Brisbane

Horse racing: Flemington Racecourse, Melbourne

Surfing: Bells Beach, Victoria; Manly Beach, Sydney; Gold Coast, QLD

"England have only three major problems. They can't bat, they can't bowl and they can't field."

Journalist Martin Johnson describing England before the 1986/87 cricket tour. England went on to win the Ashes.

14 Going Down Under

▶▶ Five best dive sites

Bourgainville Reef, QLD. Clear water and 1000-metre coral walls attracts both fish and scubbards from miles around. Boats leave from Cairns or Port Douglas.

Cod Hole, QLD. Pose with a huge maori wrasse or feed a fat-lipped giant potato cod; both weighing in at up to 100 kilos. Boats leave from Cairns.

Coral Bay, Ningaloo Reef, WA. Who needs boats or even scuba gear? Walk right off the beach and paddle out over the reef.

Princess Royal Harbour, Albany, WA. A choice of shallow-water wreck dives in a huge but sheltered natural harbour.

Port Lincoln, SA. Your chance to see the great white shark's toothy smile – from the safety of a cage, naturally.

15 Alexander Technique

The Alexander Technique was developed in the late nineteenth century by Tasmanian-born Shakespearean orator Frederick Alexander, who set about ridding himself of debilitating voice loss on stage. His form of stress management sought to overcome instinctive or habitual control over his actions to enable him to cope better with performance anxiety. Highly regarded by singers, actors, dancers and musicians; Julie Andrews, Sting, John Cleese and Paul Newman have all practised the Technique.

16 Outback road etiquette

When driving desolate Outback roads it's customary to give a one-finger salute to the infrequent oncoming traffic – no, not that one-finger salute, but a briefly raised index finger from your hand draped casually over the top of the steering wheel. It might be accompanied by a barely noticeable nod, although this can be considered exertion beyond the call of duty. Any excessive movement of the hand or worse still, the arm, designates you as a fresh-off-the-plane tourist or just a plain old drongo.

17 Politics

Exchanges between Australian politicians are famously robust and never more so than during the era of Labour Prime Minister, Paul Keating (1991–97). His withering insults flung across the floor of Canberra's New Parliament House became the scourge de jour, and were of course particularly barbed when aimed at opposition leaders. The performance of one time Liberal leader John Hewson was once likened to "being flogged with a warm lettuce" while the current PM John Howard was described as "... a dead carcass, swinging in the breeze, but nobody will cut it down to replace him."

"I like [her]...and I think she liked me."

**Former Prime Minister Paul Keating's
uncharacteristically generous appraisal of the Queen**

18 Weird beasts

European colonization had a drastic effect on indigenous flora and fauna. **Hoofed animals** were unknown and the introduction of sheep and goats, horses and cattle, along with **rabbits**, prematurely turned many areas into dustbowls. The highly poisonous **cane toads**, brought in to combat a plague of greyback beetles, have no natural enemies and for thirty years have been on a relentless march from the north Queensland sugar-cane fields, southwards along the coast and across northern Australia. But today the biggest threat to the country's ecology are **feral cats** which are getting through indigenous birds and small marsupials at a devastating rate.

19 Festivals

Festival	When and where
Beer Can Regatta – beachside race with boats composed entirely of beer cans	▶▶ July, third Sunday; Darwin
Henley-on-Todd Regatta – wacky races in bottomless boats down the dry bed of the Todd River	▶▶ October, third Saturday; Alice Springs
Laura Aboriginal Dance Festival – electrifying celebration of Aboriginal culture.	▶▶ June in odd numbered years; Laura, QLD
Australian Grand Prix – Formula 1 street racing	▶▶ March, first or second weekend; Albert Park, Melbourne
International Film Festival – lock yourself in for two weeks of celluloid heaven	▶▶ mid-June; State Theatre, Sydney
Birdsville Races – Two days of horse races followed by the clatter of 50,000 empty beer cans	▶▶ September, first weekend; Birdsville, QLD
Melbourne Cup – The entire country stops for this 146-year-old horse racing event	▶▶ November, first Tuesday; Melbourne
Sydney-Hobart Yacht Race – Crowds flock to the harbour to witness the start of this classic regatta	▶▶ December, Boxing Day; Sydney Harbour

20 Dingo de-fence

Many have heard of the Rabbit-Proof Fence (or at least the film of that name) but the 5300-kilometre **Dingo Fence** is thought to be the world's longest. Built 120 years ago to keep the indigenous wild dogs away from the vulnerable sheep flocks in the southeast of the country, it was only ever partly successful.

"To live in Australia permanently is rather like going to a party and dancing all night with one's mother "

Barry Humphries

21 Music

▶▶ Five top Australian bands and musicians

Kylie
Nick Cave and the Bad Seeds
AC/DC
Midnight Oil
INXS

▶▶ Five great Australian rock albums

Back in Black, **AC/DC**: Albert Records, 1980
Business As Usual, **Men At Work**: CBS, 1981
Kick, **INXS**: WEA, 1987
Highly Evolved, **The Vines**: Capitol Records, 2002
Diesel and Dust, **Midnight Oil**: CBS, 1987

22 Inventions

▶▶ Five Australian inventions

The Story of the Kelly Gang, made in 1906, is regarded as the world's **first feature length** film. It ran for over an hour.

The Combine Harvester, which both stripped and collected grain was developed in 1882 by Victorian farmer Hugh McKay.

Permaculture, a holistic system for human habitation based around sustainable and integrated environmental practises was developed by Bill Mollison from the 1970s onwards.

The **black box flight recorder** was invented in 1958 by Dr David Warren at the Aeronautical Research Laboratories in Melbourne.

The **freestyle swimming stroke** (originally called the "Australian Crawl") was adopted by swimmers in Sydney in the early 1900s. Its most famous female exponent was Fanny Durack who in 1912 won an Olympic gold medal, in the process cutting four seconds of the men's world record.

23 Staying alive

Australia's ecology and wildlife remain among the most distinctive on earth; it also harbours some of the world's deadliest creatures. **Crocodiles** come in two types; the misleadingly named saltwater or **estuarine crocodile** can grow to 7m, ranges far inland (often in freshwater), and is the only Australian animal that constitutes an active threat to humans; the smaller, shy, inoffensive **freshwater crocodile** feeds on fish and frogs. Three quarters of the world's most venomous **snakes** can be found in Australia – although the small number of people that actually dwell in prime snake habitats means that India experiences thousands more fatalities a year. Two spiders whose bites can be fatal are the **Sydney funnel-web**, a black, stocky creature found in the Sydney area, and the small **redback**, a relative of the notorious black widow of the Americas, usually found in dark, dry locations all over Australia (i.e outdoor toilets, under rocks and timber logs). The tropical coastal waters attract venomous **box jellyfish** during the summer months, these are saucer-sized jellyfish with long tentacles up to 3m long, whose venom can cause rapid unconsciousness and, in severe cases, paralysis of the heart muscles. Avoid swimming in tropical beaches during the **stinger season**, roughly October to May. Finally, you are more likely to be killed by bee sting or drown while surfing than be killed by shark attack in Australia.

 ## 24 Five useful words ending in "o"

Arvo – afternoon
Drongo – fool, pillock
Garbo – refuse or garbage collector
Smoko – short break from work
BYO – bring your own (alcohol to a restaurant)

25 Australia in film & TV

▶▶ Five great films set in Australia

Babakiueria (Julian Pringler, 1988). Culture-reversing spoof about Aboriginal colonizers coming ashore to disrupt a beachside "barbecue area".

Muriel's Wedding (P.J Hogan, 1994). Set in fictional Porpoise Spit on the less fictional Gold Coast, Toni Collette made her big screen debut in this pre-Kath and Kim satire on the ghastlier side of suburban Australia.

Picnic at Hanging Rock (Peter Weir, 1975). Three young ladies mysteriously disappear on Valentine's Day 1900 while on a school outing. The disturbing sense of eeriness aided by a Gheorghe Zamfir's panpipe soundtrack.

Wake in Fright (aka "Outback"; Ted Kotcheff, 1970). Deliverance Downunder; a teacher can't escape a beer-sodden, roo-shooting, Outback-town-from-hell.

Walkabout (Nick Roeg, 1971). Dad shoots his brains out during a barbie and leaves his two kids to wander the Outback until an Aboriginal boy befriends them and leads them to safety.

▶▶ Hot spots for soap buffs

The soapy teenage angst and surfie bonhomie of *Home and Away* has long revolved around **Palm Beach** in Sydney's northern beaches, with the **Barrenjoey Lighthouse** and headland regularly in shot. **Melbourne** is famous for being the filming location of *Home and Away's* competitor, the veteran soapie *Neighbours*; Ramsay Street, Erinsborough is actually **Pin Oak Court** in Vermont South, while the cool international-hit TV series, *The Secret Life of Us* was filmed around **St Kilda**.

"I'd like to be seen as an average Australian bloke... I can't think of a nobler description of anybody than to be called an average Australian bloke."

Prime Minister John Howard

25

Ultimate
experiences
Australia
small print

ROUGH GUIDES – don't just travel

We hope you've been inspired by the experiences in this book. To us, they sum up what makes Australia such an extraordinary and stimulating place to travel. There are 24 other books in the 25 Ultimate Experiences series, each conceived to whet your appetite for travel and for everything the world has to offer. As well as covering the globe, the 25s series also includes books on **Journeys, World Food, Adventure Travel, Places to Stay, Ethical Travel, Wildlife Adventures** and **Wonders of the World**.

When you start planning your trip, Rough Guides' new-look guides, maps and phrasebooks are the ultimate companions. For 25 years we've been refining what makes a good guidebook and we now include more colour photos and more information – on average 50% more pages – than any of our competitors. Just look for the sky-blue spines.

Rough Guides don't just travel – we also believe in getting the most out of life without a passport. Since the publication of the bestselling Rough Guides to **The Internet** and **World Music**, we've brought out a wide range of lively and authoritative guides on everything from **Climate Change** to **Hip-Hop**, from **MySpace** to **Film Noir** and from **The Brain** to **The Rolling Stones**.

Publishing information

Rough Guide 25 Ultimate experiences
Australia Published May 2007 by Rough Guides
Ltd, 80 Strand, London WC2R 0RL
345 Hudson St, 4th Floor,
New York, NY 10014, USA
14 Local Shopping Centre, Panchsheel Park,
New Delhi 110017, India
Distributed by the Penguin Group
Penguin Books Ltd,
80 Strand, London WC2R 0RL
Penguin Group (USA)
375 Hudson Street, NY 10014, USA
Penguin Group (Australia)
250 Camberwell Road, Camberwell,
Victoria 3124, Australia
Penguin Books Canada Ltd,
10 Alcorn Avenue, Toronto, Ontario,
Canada M4V 1E4
Penguin Group (NZ)
67 Apollo Drive, Mairangi Bay, Auckland 1310,
New Zealand

Printed in China
© Rough Guides 2007
No part of this book may be reproduced in
any form without permission from the publisher
except for the quotation of brief passages in
reviews.
80pp
A catalogue record for this book is available
from the British Library
ISBN: 978-1-84353-815-8
The publishers and authors have done their
best to ensure the accuracy and currency of
all the information in **Rough Guide 25 Ultimate
experiences: Australia**, however, they can
accept no responsibility for any loss, injury, or
inconvenience sustained by any traveller as
a result of information or advice contained in
the guide.

1   3   5   7   9   8   6   4   2

Fly Less – Stay Longer!

Rough Guides believes in the good that travel does, but we are deeply aware of the impact of fuel emissions on climate change. We recommend taking fewer trips and staying for longer. If you can avoid travelling by air, please use an alternative, especially for journeys of under 1000km/600miles. And always offset your travel at www.roughguides.com/climatechange.

Rough Guide credits

Editor: Karoline Densley
Design & picture research: Jess Carter
Cartography: Katie Lloyd-Jones,
Maxine Repath

Cover design: Diana Jarvis, Chloë Roberts
Production: Aimee Hampson,
Katherine Owers
Proofreader: Megan McIntyre

The authors

Chris Scott (Experiences 1, 3, 4, 5, 7, 8, 9, 10, 11, 14, 15, 16, 17, 19, 22, 23, 24, 25, Miscellany) is the co-author of the Rough Guide to Australia.
Lucy Ridout (Experiences 2, 21) is a freelance writer and an author of several Rough Guides.
Anne Dehne (Experience 6) lives in Australia and is the co-author of the Rough Guide to Australia.
Alec Simpson (Experiences 12, 18, 20) lives in Melbourne and writes travel features for a motorcycling magazine.
Martin Dunford (Experience 13) is co-author of World Party: the Rough Guide to the World's Best Festivals.

Picture credits

Cover Uluru at sunset © Glen Allison/Getty

2 Artist at work in the Central Desert © Frans Lanting/Corbis

6 Gas pump © Carl Purcell/Corbis

8–9 Mossman Gorge, Daintree National Park © Theo Allofs/zefa/Corbis; palm leaf © Rainforest Agencies/istockphoto; white-lipped tree frog © Tim Graham/Alamy; swimming in Daintree National Park © sack.to/istockphoto; ringtail possum © FrithFoto/Bruce Coleman Inc./Alamy; kayaking in the Daintree Forest © Chris McLennan/Alamy

10–11 Watarrka National Park © Bill Bachman/Alamy; Garden of Eden, Kings Canyon © AA World Travel Library/Alamy; Kings Canyon © Deco Images/Alamy

12–13 Woman snorkelling, Qld © Mark A. Johnson/Alamy; school of fish, Qld © Mark A. Johnson/Alamy; green sea turtle, Qld © Bruce Miller/Alamy; hardyhead fish, Qld © Gary Bell/ImageState/Alamy

14–15 Revellers at the Gay & Lesbian Mardi Gras © John Van Hasselt/Corbis Sygma; woman at the Gay & Lesbian Mardi Gras © John Van Hasselt/Corbis Sygma; men in leather at Mardi Gras © Richard Glover/Corbis

16–17 Uluru, Northern Territory © Kevin Lang/Alamy

18–19 Saltwater crocodile © Paul A. Souders/Corbis

20–21 AFL match, Melbourne © Mark Dadswell/Getty

22–23 Boat shed, Cradle Mountain NP © czardases/istockphoto; cross section of a Huon Pine © Kalulu/istockphoto; Overland Track, Lake St Clair NP © Steffan Hill/Alamy

24–25 Sunrise over vineyard © Ben Goode/istockphoto; wine glass stain © Billyfoto/istockphoto; drink stains © Wadders/istockphoto

26–27 Steps to Cable Beach, Broome © Martin Norris/Alamy; Chinese Heritage Gate, Broome © Elizabeth Czitronyi/Alamy; Chinatown © David South/Alamy; camels on Cable Beach © Steffan Hill/Alamy

28–29 Sydney Opera House and Sydney

Harbour Bridge © David Wall/Alamy

30–31 Karijini National Park © Jason Friend/Alamy; Karijini Falls © Tony Yeates/Chris Scott

32–33 Surfing © David F/istockphoto

34–35 Aboriginal artist painting © Reuters/Corbis; artist at work in the Central Desert © Frans Lanting/Corbis

36–37 Outback dirt road © Claver Carroll/Alamy

38–39 Queen Victoria Market © Alec Simpson; crabs © Alec Simpson; doughnut van © Alec Simpson; shrimps © Dan Chippendale/istockphoto; mangosteens © Dystortia/istockphoto; Polish Deli Smokehouse © David Wall/Alamy; rambutans © Iain Farley/Alamy; baby squid © Sindre Ellingsen/Alamy

40–41 Kayaking at Shark Bay © Chris Scott

42–43 Helicopter flight over the Bungle Bungles © Yann Arthus-Bertrand/Corbis

44–45 White-water rafting, Franklin River © Tourism Tasmania

46–47 Telegraph road, Cape York © Tom Gardner/Alamy; Eliot Falls, Cape York © Tom Gardner/Alamy; bearded lizard © Chris Burt/istockphoto; Cooktown © CSI Productions/Alamy; gas pump © Carl Purcell/Corbis; Oodnadatta Track © iTobi/istockphoto

48–49 Diver and whale shark © Jeff Rotman/Alamy; whale shark at Ningaloo Reef © Jeff Rotman/Corbis; whale shark © Danita Delimont/Alamy

50–51 Cattle muster, Outback © Bill Bachman/Alamy; stockman near Katherine © Patrick Ward/Alamy; camp breakfast in the Outback © Bill Bachman/Alamy; Outback pub © Bill Bachman/Alamy

52–53 Art installation, Adelaide Festival © David Moore/Alamy; road sign, Adelaide Fringe Festival © Iain Masterton/Alamy; street performer © Iain Masterton/Alamy

54–55 Whitsunday Islands © Peter Fakler/Alamy; aerial view over the Whitsundays © MagicMix/istockphoto

56–57 View from the Ghan train © Suzy Bennett/Alamy

58 Camp breakfast in the Outback © Bill Bachman/Alamy

Over 70 reference books and hundreds of travel
guides, maps & phrasebooks that cover the world

Index

ROUGH GUIDES Australia

ROUGH GUIDES Cuba

ROUGH GUIDES Britain

ROUGH GUIDES Singapore

ROUGH GUIDES Vietnam

ROUGH GUIDES New York City

ROUGH GUIDES